POTTED PORTRAITS

Verse Vignettes of Twenty One
Remarkable Historical Personalities

Christopher Rose

Illustrated by Claire Venables

Matador
Unit E2 Airfield Business Park,
Harrison Road, Market Harborough,
Leicestershire. LE16 7UL
Tel: 0116 2792299
Email: books@troubador.co.uk
Web: www.troubador.co.uk/matador
Twitter: @matadorbooks

ISBN 978 1805140 115

British Library Cataloguing in Publication Data.
A catalogue record for this book is available from the British Library.

Printed and bound by CPI Group (UK) Ltd, Croydon, CR0 4YY
Typeset in 10pt Minion Pro by Troubador Publishing Ltd, Leicester, UK

Matador is an imprint of Troubador Publishing Ltd

For Andrew and Helen

CLEOPATRA VII
(69 BC – 30 BC)

Some suppose – have they seen her nose? –
The Egyptian queen a cutie;
Cleopatra lacked, as a matter o' fact,
Strong claim to facial beauty.
If for the screen she'd shot a scene,
Especially the trailer,
The punters mightn't have been keen –
Much better cast Liz Taylor.
[No wonder purists are annoyed
By misleading portrayals
That get put onto celluloid,
Distorting truth for sales].
Yet presence and allure, for sure,
She had – both Julius Caesar
And later on Mark Antony
Did all they could to please her.

Becoming queen when just eighteen
[A detail of her story a-
Kin to one much later seen
In that of Queen Victoria],
She'd had to wed her half-brother
[Compared to her, a dummy];

No kids with him –
Though by Caesar and Antony a mummy.

A Ptolemaic queen, she'd speak,
As all her line before her, Greek;
But quite unlike her predecessors
Learned Egyptian – and she'd dress as
Rulers in Pharaonic days –
The masses gave masses of praise;
They thought Queen Cleo was terrific
Mastering the hieroglyphic.
Her half-brother might have thought
The studious efforts of this sort
A waste of time, enquiring, 'Why, sis,
All this emphasis on Isis?'

If appraisal of her nasal
Feature's not the best;
In physiognomy, as it may be, one hardly blest,
Her face would grace the coinage,
That at least with it impressed.
She innovated here:
Coins of base metal had fixed worth –
In other words, 'face value' –
There, of ironies, no dearth!
Her reign was not untroubled;
Plots were thick upon the ground;
With dangerous threats it bubbled
While her siblings were around.
[Of course a plot, however thick,

Would find it hard to match
Her half-brother – you couldn't pick
A thicker from the batch].
In light of such emergencies
And urgencies of state,
The help she got from Caesar
Would be hard to overrate.
When she'd been made an exile
From her Alexandrine court
And travelled up the Nile awhile
So she might not be caught,
The strength that she'd alone lack,
She in Caesar had then found;
He'd help her get her throne back
And would turn her fortunes round:
A Roman arm to lean upon
That Roman arms might lend –
Caesar's assassination would bring all this to an end.

To bypass guards called for a plan
To reach the man she needed –
And, dressed up as a fisherman,
In this she had succeeded.
A faithful eunuch helping her, to Caesar's marbled halls
She was smuggled in a carpet – you'd say both of them had guts!
A rabbit from a hat is magic that is often seen;
Comparatively rare that where a carpet sprouts a queen…
No sooner Caesar sees her, he's a man completely sold:
Quite rapt as soon as she's unwrapped… or should that be 'unrolled'?

In Egypt's civil war she saw
One long-held wish fulfilled
When Ptolemy [the 13th] had [unluckily?] been killed.
Her power re-established, for a little while at least,
She'd care for young Caesarion –
Whose dad was soon deceased.
With Caesar dead, Rome had instead
Octavian as ruler;
Though Caesar's nephew, one with whom
Relations were much cooler.
Cleo's son, for one, a reason
She would have to go;
Another was Mark Antony,
Who had become her beau.
[As said already, Cleo didn't look much like Liz Taylor,
In which regard the cinema'd
Been something of a failure.
Where Cleo's lover is concerned, again we may be certain
There's no substantial evidence he looked like Richard Burton].

In desperate defiance and alliance had now been
The soldier statesman *manqué* and the great Egyptian queen.
Complete defeat of Tony's fleet
Saw it sink with his hopes
At Actium – the fact was that their pact was on the ropes.
In their despair, the golden pair,
Aware the game was through,
Had different approaches as to what was best to do:
Mark Antony fought on – but with hope gone, fell on his sword,
And

To seek Octavian's mercy Cleopatra he implored.
As ever proud, Cleo avowed she'd not bear such disgrace;
When next she saw Octavian, she punched him in the face.
Then, fleeing to her sealed chamber, readied for the end:
For her last meal upon this earth she now would calmly send.

Already weak from self-made wounds, a plate of figs was brought;
Within the dish [meeting her wish – she'd given this some thought]
An asp, which to her breast she'd clasp,
Its poisoned bite to be
A herald of her final gasp
And immortality.

The Dynasty with Cleo closed;
She was the final Ptolemy.
By some it might well be supposed
She'd said 'There's none to follow me.'
That was of course the simple fact,
It's clearly understood –
But after such a classy act,
Who really ever could?

THE DUKE OF WELLINGTON
(1769 – 1852)

Arthur Wellesley, Dublin born,
Replied to those who said with scorn
That thus an Irishman was he
Did no more follow logically
Than claiming that someone perforce
Born in a stable was a horse –
A put down that appears to catch
The mettle of the man who'd match
Napoleon himself; and who
Would win the day at Waterloo.*
While some insist this was a fluke, a
Triumph mainly due to Blücher,
Still, his skill had been made plain
Through earlier generalship in Spain;
His sallies there, despite repulse, a
Succour to the 'Spanish Ulcer'.
India was somewhere too
Where he had shown what he could do;
An army life he'd there begin
After he'd burnt his violin.

* Though perhaps more to his credit
Is that he might not have said it.

7

So it would appear the claim
That Wellington deserves his fame
Is quite in order – as were those
That served under Old Beaky's nose.
They'd seen upon the fabled field
Of Waterloo how he'd not yield;
And where, to Marshal Ney's despair,
There'd broken not one British square
Before the thousands-thundering tide
Of cuirassiers.
His country's pride,
On Wellington did Britons dote –
They'd stick him on a five pound note.
From Copenhagen had the Duke observed the battle's course;
Strange claim? The city's name the same as that of his fine horse.
For Bonaparte's complete defeat the Duke was widely *lauded*,
[Which, as a peer, seems fit, we hear] and also well-rewarded:
One gift for carrying the day,
The great estate of Stratfield Saye.
Triumphant, yet no gloater, he
Reflected that a victory
Brought melancholy at its cost
Surpassed only by battle lost.

In after years, like many peers,
To change he didn't warm;
To take one case – His Grace's face
Set firm against Reform.
The epithet of 'Iron Duke', while in the first place owed
To his resilience, was now ironically bestowed

For fitting iron shutters so his windows were not shattered
By stone-throwing protesters for whom voting rights had mattered.

Whigs, Radicals – the likes of them –
Deplored his lordship as PM;
Chartists-to-be, who'd see a future
That for working folk
Was one more liable to suit your
Average working bloke,
Attempted to bring Wellesley down
By bank runs, strikes and suchlike –
The things they did, the propertied
Were never going to much like.

The Irish Catholics, too, things – not a few things! – much resented;
Their grievance, with attendant inconvenience, they vented,
While Daniel O'Connell saw their cause well represented.
As 'uncrowned King of Ireland', so
With power enough to flaunt – set
On challenging the status quo,
He'd now throw down the gauntlet.
Faced with a threat so real,
The Duke and Peel clearly saw
No course to undertake
But changes make within the Law;
New rights to fix for Catholics or face a civil war.
Such pressures plain surely explain
The just adjustments needed,
But by all those that did oppose
The move, these went unheeded;

9

They would condemn any PM
Who to RCs conceded.
The C of E should be, cries ran,
The Church the Duke implant;
Upholding what was Anglican,
Not what was Anglicant.

He might displease reactionaries
In this case; but still true
To say at core his sympathies
Were Tory through and through;
His party colours, like his blood,
Of hue the truest blue.
As symbol of his preference
Past practice should remain,
One simply has to reference
The bed, which on campaign
He'd slept in – it was kept in
Use throughout his later years;
No need to change or rearrange,
The lesson clear appears.

In 1848, an anxious State
The Duke recruited;
To keep things orderly and straight
He seemed the one best suited.
With fear that over here,
Just as in Europe, we'd be undone
By revolution,
Wellington was put in charge of London.

[Ironically, patrolling on
The city's streets there'd be
The nephew of Napoleon
In the constabulary,
With the police, keeping the peace;
Years later, it occurred
He'd be, that of the Duke's decease,
Napoleon the Third].

Although slowed by the years a bit,
The ducal brain'd retained its wit.
His ingenuity was shown
In final service to the Throne:
The Crystal Palace, plagued by a great quantity of sparrows
[Which obviously could not be shot
With guns or bows and arrows],
Called forth a neat solution: it was Wellington's corrective
That sparrow-hawks be used,
Which proved entirely effective.
An agèd statesman now, within mortality's December,
He found the names in cabinet a problem to remember.
Through growing deafness, 'Who?
Who?' was his oft-repeated query,
And one of which his colleagues grew
Predictably quite weary.
In 1852 The Last Post sounded, for Death calls
To greatest as to least,
And he was buried in St.Paul's.

No slight upon his fame
Or memory, the fact imputes,
That most invoke his name
When speaking of their rubber boots.

JOSEPH STALIN
(1878 - 1953)

In considering dictators,
Stalin certainly must rate as
Very big in that group various
And frequently nefarious.
A leader among leaders
Like the *Duce* and the *Führer*;
One whose power was indeed as
Great, and grip upon it surer.
A short man, he was yet to tower
Over all; his fearsome power
Of a sort till then unknown –
A 'Genghis Khan with telephone'.
Given his most grisly story,
Aptly, he was born in Gori;
For the sort of life he'd live,
The town sounds a fit adjective.

'Stalin', meaning 'steel', was the name he chose to take;
His actual one, however, was in no sense quite so steely:
Like many things of earlier years that he was to forsake,
He'd opt to drop the moniker of 'Joseph Djugashvili'.
He'd quickly pick the Bolshevik group; of its number be one;
He rose to General Secretary, a post that was a key one.

Indeed, in this position Stalin only let those men in
Whose support he was assured of – it was worrying to Lenin.
'Comrade Stalin', ran his warning in that bit of Lenin's will
That is sometimes called 'The Testament' – a sort of codicil –
'Comrade Stalin' [to reprise] 'has too much power to apportion
Crucial offices, but may in this not show sufficient caution.'

But Lenin, when in time was read
This document, by then was dead;
Regrettably, those left, instead
Of letting Stalin go,
Decided he be left in post.
So Stalin really made the most
Of packing 'yes men' all the more
Within the Party, to assure
That he should carry all before
Him – that his word should be the law.
Precisely thus things were to prove, as
Trotsky's moves to thwart him,
By Stalin's sly manoeuvres,
Only banishment had brought him.
[No enemy, he'd grimly teach
Through Trotsky's murder, out of reach;
And Mexico was no safe place
With Stalin's agents on the case:
The last of the 'Old Guard' to cull,
He'd get an ice pick through his skull].

Total power in his grip,
He'd never let it from him slip.
Orwell captures every trait

That marks [not Marx] the Stalin state:
Totalitarian, all controlling
Arbitrary, frightening;
The leader [*vohzd*] extolling,
As his grip was ever tightening.
None now was free and none was safe;
All feared the tyrant's ire;
While mythic propaganda
Sought to drive and to inspire.

The Five Year Plans set targets of impossible attainment,
But any shortfall brought some hapless scapegoat's swift arraignment.
Show trials, purges, gulags –
Such now formed the apparatus
On the
Apparatchik's dangerous path to greater Party status.
In times of such uncertainty
On one thing still could all agree:
That no one could the future fix,
Nor *count* on their apparat*chiks*.
The fate of Kirov illustrated how one, if ascendant,
Might prompt a fatal envy – all were shown they were dependent
On the 'Red Tsar' in the Kremlin,
He whose will was Soviet Law;
At once, architect and gremlin
Of the state he oversaw.
Building up, he'd then devour;
Smiling, while his mind rehearsed
Using fear's corrosive power
To bring forth the best and worst.

In torments of uncertainty,
Alone, he knew the truth:
Behind his iron curtain, he
Was question-setting sleuth.
What reasoning had lain behind
The death-dealing *tsunami*
Of fearful executions in the ranks of the Red Army?
Where would the next conspirator or saboteur be found?
The 'wrecker' taking foreign gold, by Stalin run to ground?

No artist, no musician, was from Stalin's ire immune.
Dmitri Shostakovich found that Stalin called the tune.
Support was Life, and censure Death;
All Law, a whim capricious;
A monster pulling levers,
The 'default' of which was 'vicious'.

With cynical self-interest, he had made a callous pact
With Hitler's Nazi Germany, to spare his being attacked.
[In fairness, this was only after trying to get the West
To join an anti-fascist front, but it was unimpressed].
The Great and Patriotic War, as World War Two is known
To Russians to this day, saw Adolf Hitler overthrown.
Success many assess, when after years attained, was thanks
In no small part to victories achieved by Russian tanks,
Which only were available to thus so serve the nation
By dint of the remarkable industrialisation,
Which arguably depended on the brutal liquidation
Of the
Kulaks in the process of forced collectivization –

A programme which was pushed through by the ruthless will of Stalin,
[A policy which made him, of the Leftists, quite the darlin'].

The postwar era saw the Soviet empire grow apace,
With much of eastern Europe locked in Stalin's cold embrace.
By 1949, with help from spies and Marxist 'comrades',
The Russians had the A Bomb – so less likely US bomb raids.
A weapon gained by Russia – yet
Within her borders lurked a threat,
So Stalin said; he did employ a
Still more heightened paranoia,
Finding in all those around
Some frequently outlandish ground
[Which propaganda would expound]
For being their destroyer.
The logical conclusion was to be The Doctors' Plot,
The fanciful delusion [of the many Stalin got],
That there was a conspiracy of Zionist physicians
Which aimed to wipe out all the senior Soviet politicians.
His cure was of a lethal and predictable description;
But death prevented him from writing out his grim prescription.
He'd die a few days shy of Caesar's fateful Ides of March:
Removed, the system's linchpin and the key-stone from the arch.
By chance, his fateful summons came [none to its knock is deaf]
Upon the same day it would claim Sergei Prokofiev.
From one who'd kept such artists and composers in firm tether,
Death brought a liberation – now they'd decompose together.

MARTIN LUTHER
(1483 - 1546)

The stance he took was not a stunt,
He held his views sincerely.
He didn't start a Protestant,
Though he became one, clearly.
An Augustinian friar first,
A Saxon somewhat forceful;
In Canon Law and scripture versed;
In argument, resourceful.
It's said that Martin Luther
Owed the scale of his success
In very large part to the
Power of the printing press.
The state of German politics
Pertaining at the time
Is something else within the mix
That helped his prospects climb.

It's clear that Luther's Theses
Were among the crucial pieces
In the scheme and fomentation
Of the German Reformation.
Ninety five of them there'd been –
He'd nailed them up at Hallowe'en

[The one in 1517]
Where they were likely to be seen.

He didn't think to make a stink
That would incense the Pope;
He'd soon, though, go beyond the brink,
With views outside the scope
Of those with which there was a hope
That any Pope might cope.
But since salvation was his goal,
His sole concern concerned his soul.
No human being could atone
For sin, nor any deed
Upon their part; but God alone
As saviour could succeed.
So Luther's way – *sola fide* –
Would win no papal *bonne chance*;
There came the day Luther would pay
A high price for his conscience.

He had an earthy mode of speech;
He didn't mince his words,
Proclaiming much the Church did teach
Was strictly for the birds.
He'd not indulge Indulgences –
Exposed them as a racket:
A means by which the Papacy
Unjustly made a packet.
Though knowing there'd a quarrel be
Still, morally, he thought

He had a duty to refute
A practice of this sort.

How would the Roman Church react
Given the fact Luther attacked
So much of what the Holy See
Saw as its core theology?

The Holy Roman Emperor and Pope, for once at one,
Agreed that on the Luther issue something should be done.
The Diet of Worms this front confirms
[Though slow they'd been to action],
Demanding Luther make, for his own sake,
A full retraction.
[The Diet of Worms, if put in terms
Of one that was comestible,
Would then have been by Luther seen
As highly indigestible].
Before the court he could but stand
And show himself unbowed;
Nor by the Papal Bull unmanned,
But equally uncowed.

A Saxon, the attacks on Luther
Prompted the Elector,
Frederick the Wise, to don the guise
Of his subject's protector.
It can't be said Elector Fred
Was for religious schism;
None more than he, though,

Could be more pro
Particularism.
His goal was more control –
It then was something of a trend –
No matter Luther's views, he'd choose
To use him for this end.
To his
Fastness of the Wartburg
[Frederick's castle] as they say,
To be sure he'd not be caught,
Luther was 'spirited away'.
Close on a year he would be here,
Ten weeks of which he spent
[Just ten!]
Doing a German text of the New Testament.
If Greek one didn't speak,
He'd done a service to decrypt;
But did it make it less opaque
In German gothic script?

Luther's clash with Rome some saw
As one cause of The Peasants' War –
A perfect opportunity
To challenge *all* authority.
No natural rebel, Luther, though –
He wrote a pamphlet that would show
How keen he was to see suppressed
Rebellious peasants – who'd have guessed?

His differences with Zwingli
Quite insuperable would prove;
On the 'Real Presence' singly,
Neither one of them would move.
A case like theirs seemed splitting hairs
On such fine points as these;
But Luther saw it German chalk
To Zwingli's own Swiss cheese.

Beside that of John Calvin,
Luther's life with laughter brims;
He found a potent salve in
Music, writing twenty hymns.
A married man, he saw no ban in scripture to endorse
The unwed priest – one cause at least of his and Rome's divorce.
Some labelled him the Anti-Christ, with bitter criticism
Of Brother Martin and his part in bringing on a schism.
But if we go by Luther's word, the Devil couldn't think well
Of one who'd given him the bird and chucked at him an inkwell.
A German nationalist and anti-Semite, he might seem
A *mensch* surely to censure rather than accord esteem.
He showed what moral conscience without compromise might cause:
No 'split-the-difference' man – so different splits there'd be, and wars.

For many, 'death or nation' Reformation would entail
A compromise at last: did it succeed or did it fail?
In truth, should Luther be one who's respected or derided?
Just like the Church he left so cleft – opinion is divided.

HORATIO NELSON
(1758 - 1805)

As admirals go, Lord Nelson clinches
Quite a few more column inches
Than his fellow naval bods:
The Jupiter among the gods.
While still alive, junkets and fêtings
In his honour showed his ratings
With the general public – who,
If pressed, found they were ratings too.

When only twelve, he'd gone to sea,
Discovering once there
A permanent propensity
To suffer *mal-de-mer*.
But notwithstanding such a blight
For one whose home's the ocean,
Young Nelson's star continued bright
And brought rapid promotion.
Not pressed as crew,
He didn't view
The Navy as one trapped in.
His rise was fast
Before the mast:
By twenty he'd made Captain.

His wilful streak was seen when, just a teen, as few would dare,
Out on the ice he'd gone and taken on a polar bear.
When asked why he should ever try
To do so, he made known
His aim to win the creature's skin,
With no thought for his own.

The war with France
Gave him a chance
For daring innovation;
His novel tactics would enhance
His standing and his station;
He started to acquire
A yet higher
Reputation.
He lost an arm in Tenerife,
In Corsica, an eye;
He'd earlier had malaria,
From which some thought he'd die.
Off Cape St Vincent,
Disregarding wilfully his orders,
He forced a ship's surrender
When he led a raid by boarders.
A brilliant move again he'd prove
He could bring off in style,
Winning the day
At Aboukir Bay
[Or Battle of the Nile].

28

While previously in Naples,
Emma Hamilton he'd met;
Though already wed to Fanny,
Upon Emma he was set.
No idle fling – this thing
Would not a brief romantic sojourn be;
A baby named Horatia was the resulting progeny.
Of this fair daughter Nelson thought a
Lot – and so he tried
For her and for her mum
A decent sum
To set aside.
[Requests Nelson had made that the State paid
Something *ex gratia,*
Upon his death, to Emma Hamilton and to Horatia
Were disregarded – very far did
This leave Emma short;
Within a web of deepening debt
She found that she was caught.
And so, although the daughter
Sought a husband and did well,
Her mother – unacknowledged by her –
Ever lower fell.
Horatia a happy life lived out;
Emma did not;
No splendid end did her attend:
She died a sorry sot].

While such as I don't wish to try –
So much as smell a hope –

To kill the tale of the blind eye
Put to the telescope,
'I see no ships,' was never said
On that supposed occasion.
Defective vision still had led
To quite signal evasion:
Though Nelson knew command was made
He break off from pursuing so,
Upon his partial sight he played
As get-out for not doing so.

Constraints of space dictate no place
Can now be given here
Of all that Nelson did
In his illustrious career.
The Battle of Trafalgar
Brought his triumph and his death;
He'd beat the French and Spanish fleet,
But draw his final breath.
His tactical prowess would prove a
Winner in a key manoeuvre
Where, with daring judgement fine,
He split the Franco-Spanish line.
Decked out in decorations,
Out on deck,
He'd not that far get –
For snipers at their stations
Quickly marked him as a target.
[It's now assumed a shrapnel wound
The Admiral did slay;

A musket ball too small to cause it –
So the experts say].

Between the *Victory*'s oaken boards
He lay as battle raged;
Amid the shot and clashing swords,
He heard of ships engaged.
At last he knew the day was won;
He saw his duty had been done.
The signal had before been made
Of what England expected –
None
More True to it than Nelson stayed,
Or better it reflected.
As Hardy kissed his forehead,
So Death came now to embrace him.
Yet Nelson's memory will not fade,
For Time cannot efface him.
A hero to his countrymen,
As in that moment solemn,
Within the sounding of Big Ben,
He stands upon his column.

GIUSEPPE MAZZINI
(1805 - 1872)

Mazzini lifelong worked to see
The unity of Italy.
Although a cause that some derided,
He'd no doubt that, while divided,
It could never once expect
To have the slightest self-respect.
Thus he always firmly chided
Those who questioned as to why did
Such things matter; he was sure
His homeland would be weak and poor
Until it learned cooperation
Operating as one nation.
So it was his burning vision
To be rid of such division,
Linking the peninsula
Through thinking far less insular.
His dream and scheme was to create
From all its separate parts, one state;
To join its regions in one goal
Of making what was fractured, whole;
That Rome, Milan and Venice might
In common cause take up the fight
To end their foreign occupation,

Thus establishing a nation.
It was his avowed intent to
Foster *Il Risorgimento*.
[That is not, I know, a rhyme,
But kindly let it go this time].
Mazzini wrote, gave many a speech,
Attempted every heart to reach
As well as each Italian head –
But little of his work was read
By people of the general sort,
Who couldn't read, since never taught.

So with hopes afire, he travelled
In his quest to build a state;
But the plots he'd sire unravelled:
National freedom had to wait.
Given many a failed rising,
It was hardly that surprising
Many came to think that he,
This founder of *Young Italy*,
Lacked even the capacity
To organise or oversee
A p...arty in a brewery.

It's true his stance on
Certain things,
Made chance of triumph slender:
He looked askance on
Having kings,
And wasn't wealth's defender.

Such attitudes, it's understood,
Were bound to make it tough
For those who wanted nationhood
But not this other stuff.
Scourge of the Catholic priesthood,
Anti-Papist since his youth –
Later he'd look further eastward
In his quest to find the truth.
Principled; a Deist too –
This added to the list
Of things that pushed away those who
Agreed with much he aimed to do,
But were more secularist;
While national revolution,
Of no matter what variety,
Was no preferred solution
Among middle class society.
And as for changes of the sort
Mazzini aimed to shepherd,
How moneyed people felt and thought,
We're taught within *The Leopard*.

The fact he often bore a frown
Regarding those who wore a crown
Was something likely to annoy
The Piedmontese House of Savoy,
For which Mazzini had scant praise,
Persisting to his final days
As one determined to rebel
Against Victor Emmanuel –

Who in due course officially
Became the King of Italy.
Mazzini may have loathed it, yet he
Had to swallow – like spaghetti –
That a Royal constitution
Was the practical solution;
Few could, or would want to give
A thought for the alternative:
A new republic – although such
Would later come, result of much
Resentment of the King, when seen he
Had connived with Mussolini.

Revolutions filled the year of 1848;
For European dynasties it was a fateful date.
But false dawn to a better morn
Of hoped-for change it proved:
Most autocrats and tyrants weren't for very long removed.
Mazzini had his moment in the turmoil and unrest;
To
Extend a new agenda
For one state he did his best
When he'd briefly tasted power
Running Rome; but soon to quench
This foredoomed heroic hour,
Back the Pope came… with the French.
Mazzini, exiled then, a shunned one,
Was abroad – again in London,
Where the days he would beguile
With friends like Kossuth and Carlyle.

Death from pleurisy in Pisa
Found him thinking bitterly
Of all the failed attempts to seize a
Better deal for Italy.
On the whole, it's pretty rotten
That he tends to be forgotten;
Garibaldi, after all,
Remains a name far more recall
[At least it's still found on their lips,
A biscuit with their PG Tips?].
Mazzini, in the cause he served
Although he showed his life he'd risk it,
Doesn't win the fame deserved –
Now surely *that's* what takes the biscuit!

GRIGORI YEFIMOVICH 'RASPUTIN'
(1869 - 1916)

Dissolute? Beyond dispute;
And why should he deny it?
Forgiveness you can't win for any sin unless you try it.
Subversive was this doctrine to insist sin be esteemed,
Since only by committing it could one then be redeemed.

'Rasputin' he? Or 'Grigori'? Should it be either/or?
A cause of some controversy, just what the first stands for.
To choose to use 'Rasputin' as his name needs explanation:
Supporters thought as free of shame this style of appellation
If it was seen just to have been a common derivation
From where he had been born: 'a crossroads' –
Simply a location.
But Grigori's detractors say it factors in how low
This debauchee: the name that he
Acquired by being so.
To balk the claim that this same name
By friends might be employed,
Why was it one the Tsar and the Tsarina would avoid?
Within their correspondence a preponderance we see,
Not of the name 'Rasputin', but 'Our Friend' and 'Grigori'.
A *starets*, wandering man of God,

Was of him one description.
His pale blue eyes could mesmerize,
Their power the prescription
For young Alexei, Tsarevitch and haemophiliac son
Of Nicholas and Alexandra [and their only one].
Uniquely could this 'holy man'
[Where doctors failed, succeeding]
Have an effect that checked
Alexei's grim internal bleeding
[So long as he'd succeeded with the Tsarevitch he'd been a
Man much needed by the Tsar – still more by the Tsarina].

Aged twelve, he had correctly named
A horse thief unsuspected –
By psychic insight, locals claimed,
The culprit was detected.
He married: seven kids;
Three lived – survival rate a common one
[In view of dad, that *any* had might seem quite a phenomenon].

Rasputin's reputation as a mystic visio*nary*
Was bolstered when, at twenty,
He had seen the Virgin Mary.
He'd left his village in the wake
Of this celestial message,
A pilgrimage to undertake
[Two thousand miles' walk he'd make],
A better life to presage.
From Greece returned,
He'd clearly learned –

Seemed cast in a new mould:
The drink and womanising, if surprising,
Put on hold.

Some aristos and peasants chose
To think of him as good;
By no means all did he appall,
As most might think he would.
[But of the life of Grigori,
Accounts conflict; it's plain to see,
Much that's been said does not agree –
There's logically a failure:
E.g., we're told he frequently
Went to a bathhouse, where he'd be
Washed down by girls; especially,
They'd soap his genitalia.
Why should he smell so, then, if clean
And washed so thoroughly he'd been?
How long, the fragrant aftermath,
Ere pong negates one's latest bath?]

Tittle-tattle to a prurient public was retailed;
With lurid and lubricious tales the country was regaled.
His close association with the Empress and her daughters
The basis soon became of stories of the lewdest sort, as
With gross acts and bizarre 'facts' packed;
Though friends dismissed them strongly,
They carried weight, at any rate with some, rightly or wrongly.
Such tales of his degenerate, corrupt and wild behaviour

Were not enough to bring him down while still seen as a saviour
By certain wealthy devotees, and while all these stayed loyal;
Nor lacking the full backing of his two supporters royal.

The Court had thought it might be best
If he was sent away,
To handle any scandal, lest
Such grew if he should stay.
But Grigori would presently return;
If reprehensible,
To the Tsarina he remained
Completely indispensable.

During The First World War, he saw
His influence extend: the Tsar away,
His wife would pay to Grigori – 'Our Friend' –
Unprecedented heed; her need
Of him unwisely great:
Upon him she'd depend to help her tend the parlous state.
Political appointments he would help to engineer;
On that of the prime minister he'd a decisive steer.
His prominence – near dominance, some felt – excited fears;
A 'Mr Fixit' who could either make or break careers.
If an approving note he wrote, or if some scheme he backed,
It went ahead: he hired and fired,
Promoted, helped or sacked.
[Not eschewing soap and water
That upon him had bestowed a

Reputation foul, and brought as-
Sociation with bad odour].

Soon to come, the day Tsardom would be given a huge kick;
Result in part of listening to the wrong sort of *moujik.*

Prince Yusupov would finish off
This *starets* turn for good –
In part out of sheer boredom [it so far is understood].
Both Romanovs and Russia, though, he felt, were surely sunk
If they were left to suffer any more of the Mad Monk.

Few deaths achieved by violent means
Have ever been enacted
That trumped all operatic scenes
In being so protracted:
He first was poisoned, next was shot;
Clubbed, whipped with chains and thrown
Into the icy Neva. A *post-mortem* had then shown
The cause of death to be one that all reason must confound:
From poison, bullets, beatings, cold, not dead –
Instead, he'd drowned.

A puzzle Grigori remains:
How ever had this guy been
So great, if taking so few pains
With basic personal hygiene?

EVA PERON – 'EVITA'
(1919 – 1952)

The show *Evita* 's based upon
The short life of Eva Peron,
Who'd win a breath of sanctity
Before her death at 33.
Enduring interest in her since
The musical does well evince;
Hers was a story to entice
Andrew Lloyd Webber and Tim Rice
Not least because such tales as this
Are sure to be good box office.

Born just after the First World War,
Eva was the fifth child;
Her family grew very poor,
And also much reviled.
If you would know why this was so,
The cause is no enigma:
Her mother was unmarried
And that carried heavy stigma.
Though mistress of a cad who had his legal brood elsewhere,
She wasn't cowed – indeed, was proud; yet Eva was aware
Of putdowns and unpleasantness, and being made to feel
The stinging hiss of prejudice – the wounds would never heal.

The hatred and disgrace she had to face, and such derision
Served as a spur to her determination and decision
To get shot of her drab life and with hands, *etcetera*, grab life;
Find ways instead to stop all this
And head for the metropolis;
Once there, to show she was as good
As any in her neighbourhood.

A magazine called *Sintonìa*
[Something like *Hello!*]
Would let the teenage Eva see a
World of glam and show;
It gave her and her teen *amigas*
All they dreamed about,
Quite guaranteeing to intrigue as
Each issue came out.

It chanced that Fate would bring a
Way out through a tango singer,
Who was touring and croonin'
Around Eva's town of Junin.
He, the answer to her prayers,
Would take her back to Buenos Aires*.

* [The rhyme that Belloc chooses – and he uses in his verse –
Pairs 'Buenos Aires' with 'stocks and shares',
'Aires' here quite short, or terse.
Of course, not all will hold with this, insisting 'Buenos *Air-es*'
Preferred should be; let's just agree –
Pronunciation varies].

An actress of ambition,
Eva showed herself adept
At improving her position,
Using those with whom she slept.
Her name became fast famous
On both radio and screen.
Now highly paid, she'd made the grade –
And played a different scene.

A charity event for earthquake victims was the setting
That gave Eva a chance of her desired husband getting.
The guest of honour,
Juan Peron, a
Man she'd set her sights upon,
Found he, once she had picked him,
Was himself an earthquake victim.

Great poverty had always been a
Major blight in Argentina;
Since it first became a state,
The wealth gap had been very great.
Addressing this most pressing need
Was Eva's mission and her creed –
And one in which she did succeed
Up to a certain point.
'The shirtless ones' worshipped her name;
To them a living saint became –
Though one many besides would blame
Far sooner than anoint.

For some, Eva may seem to be
The last word in hypocrisy:
Professing and expressing lots
Of love for all the poor have-nots,
While dressing up in jewels and furs –
Designer humbug, surely, hers?

Her tour of many a European city,
[Which in part owes
It's ongoing celebrity
To Swiss throwing tomatoes],
Saw Eva's international stardom
Reach its apogee;
She met both Franco and the Pope –
A contrast, surely…? Well, let's hope…
[Could it be seen she moved between
The Devil and The Holy See?]

'*La Razón de mi vida*'
[Her biography to date]
Grabbed many an avid reader
[Who found fiction titles great?]

During an 'appendectomy', a tumour was detected –
It was thought best that she have a test,
And also take a good long rest,
As cancer was suspected.
But seemingly untroubled, she redoubled all before
And pressed ahead instead on doing more work for the poor.

As much of this was done via the telephone receiver,
Juan hoped he'd make her take a break,
And might thereby relieve her,
By severing the wires – Ah! but try as
Well he might,
She only reconnected it,
Then kept it out of sight.

[Juan Peron was twice elected
President – not unexpected:
It was pretty tough to beat a
Man supported by Evita].

Eva's death occasioned mourning
Greater than yet seen – a
Testament to what she'd meant
To much of Argentina.
Whether such acclaim she's due,
Perhaps we'll never know;
Despite whatever else is true,
Her life made a great show.

ISAMBARD KINGDOM BRUNEL
(1806 – 1859)

A photograph, which at that time –
We're talking 1859 –
Was as a medium somewhat new,
Is apt in capturing one who
Advanced by galloping degrees
Industrial technologies.
Upon his head, a stovepipe hat;
Cigar clamped twixt his teeth;
Brunel defined the epoch that
Enshrined his self-belief.

He stands before cascades of chains,
This genius far-seeing;
Whose varied legacy remains,
Sprung from one of the greatest brains
Of any human being.
The stovepipe hat, burning cigar:
How most appropriate they are!
When seen as symbols that evoke
The funnels, tunnels,
Flame and steam,
The ash and coal and smoke;

That driving, striving, thriving era
Pushing to pull the future nearer;
Busily building, smelting, refining;
Burrowing, blasting and redefining.
Planning and spanning,
Refusing to fail;
Designing anew,
Then, with bolt, screw and nail,
Putting together,
With lathes fast-revolving,
With struts, cables, arches,
New structures evolving.
New landscapes, horizons, new dreams, new ambitions;
New ventures and challenges, projects and missions.
Of this industrial creed, High Priest, an
Overseer of ceaseless motion,
Brunel set the vast *Great Eastern*,
And *Great Britain* on the ocean.
Behemoths of steam and sail –
'Great', but trailing in their wake
Commercial fact – the bitter tale:
Cash-wise, they had been a mistake.
Yet iron hulls and screw propellors
Were the future. And as well as
Innovations here, Brunel
Constructed many a bridge as well.
There really has to be a mention
Of the elegant suspension
Bridge at Clifton; more to name are
On the Thames and on the Tamar.

Fine work done on the Great Western
Railway shows him at his best; an
Enterprise at once involving
New designs and problem solving,
Having as its culmination
At its point of termination,
Paddington, its London station.
And we do injustice to Brunel in our ignoring
His work on tunnelling –
Which, while most interesting,
Was boring.
Assisting Marc, his father,
Who was rather
Brilliant too,
Beneath the waters of the Thames,
By techniques wholly new,
A hole, newly created,
There was – fated
To be flooded;
Brunel would see the tunnel through,
Unbowed, if somewhat bloodied.
No task too hard for Isambard;
No rocks he couldn't blast;
The Box Tunnel was done well,
And astonishingly fast.
That ventures of this sort were fraught
With hazard well aware,
It's creditable that he thought
It only right he share
In any danger there might be –

And risked his life quite frequently:
A rare and fine display this
Of his guts – no empty stunt;
It illustrates the way this
Genius led things from the front.

His projects ate up money,
So it's funny to reflect
On an incident trivial
Which is comic in effect:
Performing for his children
A no doubt amusing trick,
A gold half-sovereign in his throat
Had found some cause to stick.
Thanks to his dad, the gold coin had
Eventually been shifted –
It's just as well, or for Brunel,
Fils,
This a likely funeral knell;
And we'd, so far as we can tell,
Have lost one very gifted.

You might well ask whence 'Kingdom' came –
It was his mother's maiden name.*
Why, though, bestow on him the same?
Well, which could have a better claim,
Regarding names, one might explain,
Than this to be a shared domain?

With war in the Crimea there would be a
Further chance
For one who'd done so much,
Still more solutions to advance:
Prefabricated hospitals – designed, built, sent –
Would be
A huge success – more cause to bless
The name of IKB.
At once, the numbers dying fell
And hygiene standards rose;
Scutari was replaced as well,
Few sad to see it close.
'The Lady with the Lamp' had ample praise,

* [Engaged, the 'plighted' thing done,
Was she Miss united Kingdom?
Or,
Miss Kingdom, when a bride to be –
That is to say, once plighted –
Might one then quite correctly see
As Miss Kingdom united?
United, though, while still 'Miss'? – No,
Quite inconsistent this is;
Once wed, as well, she'd be 'Brunel' –
Instead of Miss, be Mrs].

No ifs or buts;
She'd speak admiringly always
Of 'Those [amazing] huts'.

When only fifty three he died,
Succumbing to a stroke.
The pistons seized; the firebox cooled;
The funnel ceased to smoke.

NOËL COWARD
(1899 – 1973)

Epitome of English wit,
Of cigarettes urbanely lit,
In evening dress of perfect fit,
Among the fast set, faster;
Who else but Noël Coward might
Be so described? That theatre knight
Who came to be acclaimed by right
Quite simply as
'The Master'?
Composer of the songs he sings;
Director, actor, writer;
Amidst the Twenties' Bright Young Things
There surely was none brighter.
Nostalgic, caustic, funny, wry,
The wells of wit not once ran dry,
From *Private Lives* to *Sail Away*,
On stage and screen,
In film and play.
Vicissitudes of national life
Were caught within his rhymes;
Sublime his distillation
Of the nation and his times.
In Which We Serve
Could brace the nerve

And firm the spine of Britain;
While *London Pride*
Stand proud beside
Quite any song yet written.
The scintillating repartee
Of comedies still done
Show the originality,
The mirth and timeless fun
Contained – as we cannot contain our loud and *Present Laughter* –
Within the lines which will be heard down all the years hereafter.

His first appearance: Teddington* – which didn't get reviews;
But with a pushy mother and a talent to amuse,
The little Noël's
Pursuit of rôles
Was his relentless mission;
At every chance
He'd sing and dance
And turn up to audition.
A confident, precocious boy,
His stage career soon flowered;
When for producers he'd appear,
No fear that Noël cowered.
Polite refusals, need for tact –
These weren't required: he could act.
Of compliments, as mother thought, a
Most deserving son –

* Referring to his birth – he'd not
Get write-ups till an older tot.

60

Far worthier than that daughter
Of a Mrs Worthington…

He set the theatre spinning
With *The Vortex,* which did more
To make his name and bring him fame
Than anything before –
But then, that triumph came
When he was only twenty-four.
A string of hits;
Suites at the Ritz;
He found he'd rather take a
House far away
From skies of grey –
Where he'd have far less tax to pay –
And settled in Jamaica.
Across the years he'd widely roam
To other bits o' land;
Indeed, he had another lovely home
In Switzerland.
He wrote a quite specific rôle
For Gertrude Lawrence, his twin soul –
A classic instance, *Private Lives,*
In which she played one of the wives.
[A masterpiece of brittle wit,
In just three days he wrote that hit].

Of Gertie Lawrence he would say,
'She simply took my breath away.'

The wartime Forties
Brought his
Morale boosting to the fore:
In Which We Serve, This Happy Breed –
He met a very real need
With films like these, and most agreed
They'd helped to win the war.
Ill-famed *Mad Dogs and Englishmen*
In crisp, clipped tones he sang
For WAAFs and WRENS and servicemen
From Plymouth to Penang.
Performance of a different sort
He gave – though no less dry:
The Germans never thought him –
And they therefore never caught him
In the rôle the war had brought him –
As unlikely British spy.

Postwar Britain wanted gritty
Realism, not his witty
Brand of arch frivolities –
Whatever else their qualities;
The *soigné* actor of renown
Swathed in his hallmark dressing gown,
Together with his plays, was rated
More than just a little dated.

But if some stuff did less well, he
Found new fame on US telly;
And a Vegas venue showered –

Deluged – dollars down on Coward;
Seeing the stupendous fee,
He said that he'd quite happily
Have audiences groan at him
And have coke bottles thrown at him.

The Sixties mixed his
Cabaret and stage roles with the screen –
Near-cameos he chose
To keep his reputation green:
To patronise a heist enticed
In *The Italian Job*;
In *Bunny Lake Is Missing*,
A louche literary slob.
He might have taken on James Bond
As oriental foe –
But to the part of Doctor No he tartly had said 'No'.
[In casting, very often studios' choices are inscrutable;
And yet, what a regret that Coward thought himself unsuitable…]

At 70, an event he
Had longed for: quite delighted,
When by the Queen [at last!] he'd been,
For many first nights, knighted.
'Sir Noël's a phenomenon
That won't appear again',
The verdict ran of Rattigan,
And truth of which was plain.
His homosexuality
Officially was never

Acknowledged by him publicly,
And, were he questioned ever
Why 'coming out' about it
Should prove such a tricky test,
Said
He'd disappoint old dears in Worthing
Who had still not guessed.
Beside his bed,
The last thing read,
A work of childhood past:
E.Nesbit, Coward's favourite –
Sentimental to the last.

LUDWIG VAN BEETHOVEN
(1770 – 1827)

With burning eyes
And bushy brows
And wild, disordered hair,
Romanticism's pugilist
Directs at Fate his glare.
Defiant in his deafness,
Hewing from the living rock
The elemental sounds that ever
Shout and shake and shock:
The Furious, the tender;
The ebullient, comic, grave;
Now the god imposing order;
Now the imp who'll misbehave.

Presented as a prodigy,
Like Mozart and his kind;
A cash machine his father'd seen
His son as – this in mind,
His drunkard dad had beaten him
If he played a wrong note;
Financially, it soon would be
Young Ludwig who the family

Would have to keep afloat.
Though born in Bonn,
Ludwig had gone
At 22 – by then a
Fine pianist already –
Off to study in Vienna.
As Mozart was now dead,
He had instead
For lessons tried an
Illustrious alternative:
He went to Joseph Haydn.
Young Ludwig's counterpoint was honed,
If Haydn on occasion moaned
About his pupil's urge to stray
From doing things his teacher's way.
Though Haydn pride 'n joy still had
In much the lad was writing,
Beethoven thought that Haydn taught
Him nothing – pretty biting!
Considering this verdict bleak,
Which verges on abuse,
A pity he should Haydn seek,
Then find him such scant use…

An *oeuvre* of verve his claim to fame:
Some thirty-two sonatas
For pianoforte to his name –
But that is just for starters:
Nine symphonies, concertos – and lest anyone forgets,
There are sixteen quite remarkably inventive string quartets.

He soon wrote off Napoleon,
And flew into a temper – a
Hypocrite bent wholly on
A quest to be an emperor.
In rage,
The title page
From his *Eroica* he tore:
Now Bonaparte would own no part
Of his heroic score.
Beethoven stood for brotherhood –
And should you choose to doubt it,
One hearing of the *Ode to Joy*
Will set you right about it.
Though praising universal love,
His own quest would be blighted;
In social terms, too far above
Him those his heart ignited.
And so away he had to shove
All hope of love requited.
He contemplated suicide
With deafness on him closing;
But ultimately threw aside
Such thoughts, and kept composing.
His opera, *Fidelio* [the title that endures –
Leonora came before a
Change of name and overtures];
Concertos for piano, five in all:
The Fifth, *The Emperor*,
A mainstay of the concert hall,
And as some people may recall,

Performed in manner to enthral
By Barenboim and Klemperer.

It may be the fifth symphony
Is his most famous op. –
Ta ta ta TAAA –
Ta ta ta TAAA –
Arrests, but doesn't stop.
This startling start to Number Five,
Astounding, broke new ground –
Relentless in its rhythmic drive,
In one dynamic bound
It powers forward –
Rushing on, a tidal wave in sound –
On hearing it, Weber declared
He wondered how Beethoven dared
To write something, likely as not,
Which showed that he had lost the plot.

To all wise counsel deaf, few
Don't say Beethoven appears
Concerning Karl, his nephew –
Notwithstanding his dulled ears.
The young boy's custody he won,
Quite blind to the great harm he
Was doing once he had begun
As guardian – Karl had little fun;
So, no surprise to anyone
That,

Once he had the chance to run,
Karl went and joined the army.

Romantic though he may have been,
Yet quite hard-headed, too;
Beethoven's business sense was keen
Regarding monies due.
A golden coin mislaid
Had made
Him quite as mad as any –
He wrote a piece about it
Called *Rage over a Lost Penny*.

First of the great composers
Not to have a patron fixed,
His earnings you'd suppose as
A result were rather mixed.
He'd some, like Prince Lichnovsky,
As Tchaikovsky had Von Meck –
But not the kind that bind one's hands,
A millstone round the neck.

His deathbed scene
Was not serene,
But fitting of his life:
A furious storm that seemed some form
Of mighty Hymn to Strife:
The thunder, as of rolling drums,
Split open Heaven's portal;

All Nature cried 'Beethoven comes!'
He passed to the immortal.

About the *Wienerwald* perhaps his shade's seen still to wander,
And over some melodic phrase continues there to ponder.
Should you be blessed with such a guest, notating staves and clef,
Then say '*Grüss Gott, Herr Beethoven!*' Speak up – he's rather deaf.

MOHANDAS GANDHI
(1869 - 1948)

Who is that sitting cross-legged there
Within a quiet London square?
Mohandas Gandhi – just one statue
Of him, of the many that you
May encounter on the way
From here in London to Bombay*.

He left his father's sickbed,
Thence to be with his young wife –
With whom he'd then indulged the carnal side of married life.
His father's death, Mohandas later learned, had come at just
The moment that he'd been engaged in working off his lust.
His guilt at this coincidence of filial desertion
Of sick paternal parent for some sexual diversion
Would haunt him and impel him to an abstinence from sex –
A course some felt extreme,
And many more still will perplex.

To study Law, his family sent
Him off to London, where he spent
Three years – mostly a resident

* [Mumbai, that is – I'll use the name
It had when Gandhi won acclaim].

Of the East End [to save on rent].
Mohandas, with his open mind
[For prejudice of any kind
Was always something he deplored],
New ways of living had explored.
Of these, one of significance was his eschewing meat;
And chewing, in so doing, on what vegetarians eat.
This new regime had led him into contact with a few
Whose radical, progressive thinking changed his point of view.

In all his deeds the central thrust is
To apply his creed of justice;
Righting wrongs with moral sense
Without recourse to violence.
Satyagraha was evolved
That in this manner should be solved
The very stark inequities
Of Indian communities –
Effronteries with which his own compatriots he'd charge,
That touched on the Untouchables as much as on the Raj;
His training as a lawyer, which in London he'd received,
He'd later on employ a lot in helping the aggrieved.

While Gandhi's name may yet remain
Above all linked to one campaign –
The *Hind Swaraj* [in Hindi], a
Design for freeing India –
By no means was Home Rule the sole
Obsessive, all-absorbing goal

Of Gandhi's life; he frequently
Devoted time and energy
To causes in the main concerned
With how the poorest lived and earned.
The Twentieth century still unborn,
And far from in its stride,
He'd shown how he could be a thorn
In vested interests' side.
He'd face a case with race
The basis of discrimination –
Despite his ticket, made to leave a train
At the next station.
This incident spurred his intent
To see a greater fairness
In law for those who bore such blows,
And raise others' awareness.

When on an unarmed crowd, aloud came call to open fire,
The general's name sounded the same as what resulted: Dyer.
Few scenes would scar as Amritsar the record of the Raj;
Forever would its stain remain, together with the charge
Brought by the Court of History: that Britain's claim to rule
Did not have a just basis in the Empire's greatest jewel.
Where there had been a reverence for Britain's Indian mission,
A wish now keen for severance from its subject position;
For Gandhi, Congress, India, events it set in train
That told the Raj and those in charge they couldn't long remain.

He'd spin six hours a day –
Not in a way that made him dizzy;

The thinking here at play
Beyond just that of keeping busy:
By making cloth to meet his need,
He hoped for emulation
And see *Swadeshi* thus succeed
Across the Indian nation.
When protest into violence passed,
He viewed it as disaster,
And hoped by practising a fast
To slow and stem it faster.

He'd wilfully commit a crime
By making salt at Dandi –
A place name that's a gift to rhyme
With one whose name's Mohandas.
George Orwell [no Imperialist] said Gandhi fairly got
A hearing from the British in a way that he would not
From many other Powers – he would simply have been shot.

A London conference little difference
Made; but Gandhi came –
Revisiting his East End haunts,
Which still looked much the same…
Of Western civilisation, asked his view,
He'd made it clear
He thought it would, as things then stood,
Be quite a good idea.

Congress, keen not to be seen
To have revolved about him;

So great had his charisma been,
It couldn't do without him.
Acclaimed as the *Mahatma*
[Hindi, that, for 'The great Soul'],
Some nonetheless felt that far
Overpraised him and his rôle.
For these, in no sense hero and courageous agitator –
Some Nationalists regarded him as nothing but a traitor.

Partition not a winner
With him,
Gandhi was dismayed
When the
Fears of such as Jinnah
And the Muslims weren't allayed.
Once Pakistan existed
He would nonetheless display
No rancour, but insisted
It be dealt with a fair way.

A martyr to his mission he had literally become
When,
In independent India, to bullets he'd succumb.

With principles of compromise in politics required,
Should compromise of principles be equally desired?
He practised self-denial;
Showed commitment to great causes –
Far more than you 'n I'll –
Greater, too, than mine or yours is.

Self-publicist? A narcissist?
Churchill's 'half-naked fakir'?
Should these be missed from any list
Of what view we should take here?
A controversial figure still,
Clear answers not at hand, we
Most likely have some time to wait till
All agree on Gandhi.

VINCENT VAN GOGH
(1853 - 1890)

There can't be very many – are there any? –
Who would claim
Van Gogh is undeserving of his world-embracing fame.
The auction rooms, of course, endorse his art's being commercial;
To say it sells for massive sums is hardly controversial.
The arguments, it seems, do not concern his name's repute;
It's more the way you say it that appears to cause dispute.

For people writing verse, a curse this is – the safest call
As regards pronunciation's not to rhyme his name at all.
The Dutch – and as Van Gogh himself was such, it's hard to knock –
Make claim his name correctly should be given as 'Van Gogh'.
Americans in reference, though, a preference will show
[And in this they are quite alone] for calling him 'Van Gogh'.
So far as it has relevance, the prevalence in Britain
As usual's not to say it in the way it may be written:
With 'GH' at the end, an F's produced – a few may scoff –
The consequence thus being to pronounce the name 'Van Gogh'.

Though some may cast aspersions on some versions,
Or may wince,
At least the name is short – so ought that pain be they evince.
Syllabically, the name's the same – consideration chief
In using it without giving offence – a great relief.

Vincent Willem started life,
Son of a pastor and his wife,
At Zundert, 1853 –
The eldest of six children he.
The eldest child maybe, but throughout life he would depend
Upon his brother Theo right until its sorry end.
[He said that without Theo's care
He would have known complete despair,
With often not a crust for nibbling
But for his kind younger sibling].

Sent to work in London, there
The first address he fixed on
For lodgings was at 87 Hackford Road in Brixton.
The job was one of many on which Vincent made a start;
At least it was connected, as not all were, with fine art.
But salaries from galleries were really not his style;
He yearned to serve humanity in some way more worthwhile.
Rich clients met defiance in this russet-headed minion;
With art *discussed*, his own for them they heard in his opinion.
As dealer, too, his record few would probably impress;
He got transferred to Paris in the hope of more success.
But as before – indeed, still more –
His manner was abrasive;
He lacked the tact required to be patient and persuasive.
Implicit criticism of their taste did not amuse
Those who'd come to view his canvases, but not canvass his views.
From London days, he'd only praise
For Constable and Turner –
And also some of Millais'

Stuff – but still he couldn't earn a
Sufficient income from his work;
Perennially, he'd lack
A way to stay out of the red
Instead of in the black.

Van Gogh's amours were always cause
Of misery and pain;
In London he'd been undone,
As he was to be again.
To Kee – a widow – he in 1881 proposed;
Her flight in fright had not been quite
The answer he'd supposed.
His living with a prostitute
Had caused his parents shame:
Their son with one of ill-repute
A stain on their good name.
No lasting union did it prove –
A focus on career
Saw Vincent once more on the move,
Though now with gonnorrhea.
One might think a 'blue period' these trials would behove;
Van Gogh went off [Van Gogh did go…?]
To learn from one named Mauve.

In Paris he'd learnt much from the *atélier* he attended;
And several great young painters, such as Sisley, he befriended.
Fernand Cormon was *très très bon, pas question, dans chaque* session;
The French Impressionists had also made a big impression.

Between some time in Antwerp, Drenthe – or whichever location,
He homeward pressed when stressed by his financial situation;
For there he'd save what he'd have spent
On buying food or paying rent.
His dad, who too could moody grow,
Cleared space to make a studio.

Vincent had done his sunflowers; self-portraits too – there's one
Which shows him with his bandaged ear [at least it couldn't run].
The vibrant hues he'd choose to use,
Combined with brushstrokes bold,
Though later they'd get rave reviews,
In his day rarely sold.

'The Yellow House' in Arles he hoped would be a fervid hub
For fellow painters, making it a great Bohemian club.
Gaugin had gone and joined him – all went well at first, but then
There'd been an incident where Vincent lost the plot again.
As usual, Van Gogh's motive for his votive gift's unclear:
Why should a girl called Rachel want to have the painter's ear?
In fact, not the whole ear, we hear – but still it's hard to probe:
One can't claim it a typo in such show of heartfelt lobe.

His suicide hardly defied well-founded expectation;
He'd struggled with poor mental health and had a reputation
For chronic instability.
Though tragic, no surprise
When such as he decides to be the hand by which he dies.
Let's not be down – he's won renown;
His joyful *Sunflowers* ours,

Their vivid blooms his shining crown –
DON'T PUT THEM IN A VASE! *

* if US English speech one has,
This last rhyme might well faze;
Please read this last injunction as:
'DON'T PUT THEM IN A VASE!'

WINSTON CHURCHILL
(1874 – 1965)

Class warriors might condemn him
For his being born at Blenheim.
But even as that may be,
Winston Churchill as a baby
Had no power to avoid
The privilege that he enjoyed;
Nor have the very slightest say
Upon his birth in any way
[As no one has in any age
In matters of their parentage].

Adoring of his parents, they
Would rarely give him time of day.
Lord Randolph's attitude was one
Of distance to his elder son;
While Winston's mother, somewhat better,
Sometimes wrote her son a letter
When he was at Harrow boarding –
Not a time he found rewarding.*

* A book by John and Celia Lee
Reveals a closer family
Than that more usually suggested –
Read it, if you're interested.

Sandhurst was his cup of tea;
He got into the cavalry.
And polo he came to adore –
He played it out in Bangalore.
As journalist, he'd many capers
Covering wars for sundry papers.
Captured, he won great applause
By then escaping from the Boers.
He'd made a name; his fame quite sold 'em
On him when he stood for Oldham,
Whose electors promptly sent
Young Winston into Parliament.
A Tory, as his Pa before,
He felt he had to cross the floor
And Liberal be, a change he made
Upon the issue of free trade.
Within the Cabinet before
The outbreak of the First World War,
He'd by that time risen to be
The First Lord of the Admiralty.
Among the Great War's many hells,
That centring on the Dardanelles
Brought terrible humiliation,
And, indeed, his resignation.
Back to frontline service, then:
Winston was at war again.
Despite leading a busy life,
At 33 he'd found a wife.
Although by no means all serene,
This marriage to his Clementine

Would last his life's remaining length
And prove a vital source of strength.
Between the wars,
He found alarming
Nazi Germany's rearming;
For all Hitler's guarantees meant,
Most uneasy with appeasement.
What a dreadful shame Berlin
Had only Neville Chamberlain
To deal with. So Munich came,
An episode of national shame:
Was ever there a deal tackier?
Selling out Czechoslovakia!
With his warnings vindicated,
Churchill soon was elevated
To the premiership and power
In the country's darkest hour.
Just the person people thought he
Was to have in 1940.
One of oratory's true giants,
Churchill's speeches growled defiance.
Making common cause with Russia,
Here he saw the need to usher
In a time of joint decisions,
Overcoming past divisions.
To the many who complained,
He made his case when he explained:
If Hitler had invaded Hell,
He'd even wish the Devil well.

Under peril of invasion,
Britain rose to the occasion.
Churchill sensibly had felt
From early on that Roosevelt
Should be persuaded to extend
A helping hand; so Lease and Lend
Threw out a lifeline,
Gladly grasped;
Then in the US came at last.

With the public's next selection
At the General Election,
Churchill found himself rejected,
In an outcome unexpected.
Clementine herself assessing
It a blessing
In disguise,
'Most effectively disguised',
Was Churchill's comment – otherwise
He might discern more easily and readily the root
Of why he'd been presented with The Order of the Boot.

Close on fourscore, PM once more,
By him was overseen
A change of monarch from King George the Sixth
To the new Queen.
He painted, won a Nobel Prize, was reverenced by the masses;
You'd often spot
Him on the yacht
Of host, Ari Onassis.

On turning 80, Parliamentary colleagues of his motherland
Presented Churchill with his portrait, done by Graham Sutherland.

'A remarkable example', he declared
'Of modern art';
[Though that verdict's double-edged, he frankly loathed it from the start:
'An old man at his stool',
Was how he'd privately described it,
With other comments cruel –
He had effectively proscribed it.
From hitherto entirely secret sources it's now learnt
That, on Clementine's instructions,
The detested thing was burnt].
The great man's final years were not ones happy or fulfilling;
Acceptance of declining powers found Churchill most unwilling.
He liked Gilbert and Sullivan, and often played bezique;
But more and more withdrew from life: would watch, but seldom speak.
Modest was his grave at Bladon
Set against the send off laid on;
None alive then could recall
A more impressive funeral.
Beyond doubt, a colossus he,
Who'd carried safe to victory
The cause of freedom; strong his claim
To wide renown and lasting fame.
So celebrate him with Hurrah!
And give the man a big cigar!

NAPOLEON B[U]ONAPARTE
(1769 - 1821)

Napoleon must top the lists
Of History's great *arrivistes*.
Although his blood was faintly blue,
He still was thought a *parvenu*
By those who felt a throne apart
From that of any Bonaparte.

[A curious fact, his year of birth
Was Wellington's first one on Earth –
Akin to Hardy's poem, *The convergence of the twain*,
In which, unwitting, grow the ship
And iceberg, that its hull will rip;
Both nemesis and doomed to slip
One day their fateful rein.
NB. another one – and that's
NB's abiding fear of cats;
You wouldn't see him make a bee-line
For a purr-y, furry feline.
Being keen on bees and eagles
Didn't mean he worshipped beagles].

Can he be judged a self-made man,
This Corsican? Of course 'e can!
But surely few shall disagree
That luck was crucial, and that he
Though self-made, still the sort that makes
More of himself through lucky breaks.
As Corsican at source, a language course, of course he'd need;
Command of French command of France quite clearly must precede.
At nine years old he was enrolled,
To learn it, then was back sent;
He passed all his exams, we're told,
But never got the accent.
The Revolution served him well:
'A whiff of grapeshot' was a smell
His masters felt quite hit the spot
By hitting many *sans-culottes*.
Promotion from commotion came;
He rapidly made quite a name –
Indeed, he quite re-made his own:
He'd soon as 'Bonaparte' be known;
Perhaps appropriate to do,
As this now made his name 'non-U'
In an egalitarian time,
And might facilitate his climb.
Apart from this, a French battalion
Wouldn't think he was Italian.

He doted on his Josephine, though she sought love elsewhere;
But later on, her lover gone, for him she came to care.
The teeth she didn't lack were black, which hardly sounds that glamorous;

Indeed be thought rather to thwart success in ventures amorous.
But it was not her dentistry that finally would force
The hard-headed Napoleon to fix on their divorce:
Her age precluded any hope of giving him a son,
And for the future dynasty Napoleon needed one.
With younger wife, the regime's life acquired prospects fair;
A window would be opened thus to get a little heir.

A brilliant self-publicist, he took great pains to see
His exploits on campaign weren't missed while based in Italy.
Reports were thus created, calculated to enhance
Napoleon's reputation with the public back in France.
To take but one example of the myths that he would peddle
And how with truth Napoleon without a doubt did meddle:
Upon a steed of white his Alpine crossing was portrayed;
That's not indeed quite right, as on a mule it had been made.

A well-read and a cultured man, Napoleon from the start
A kleptomaniac spree began with other countries' art.
Great canvases and treasures were now lost to their descendants;
Venetians saw their bronzes go – and then their independence.
Small wondering this plundering those under him would prove
A source of much resentment of Napoleon, and the *Louvre*.

The coup he carried through came at the foggy time of year:
Brumaire – but what he aimed to do thereby was pretty clear.
The Consulate was but a pro. tem. partner in the dance
For one who's on a mission his ambition to advance,
And sees a way to seize the day and Caesar play in France.

Although we know he did declare
That merely an upholstered chair
And nothing more is all a throne is,
Still he gave them to his cronies,
Judging that their royal rank,
For which they'd all have him to thank,
Would mean he'd have a firmer hold
On all the states that he controlled.
In fact he found some didn't do
Precisely what he told them to:
His brother, Louis, ruled the Dutch
And felt his loyalties as such
Should firstly be to Holland's cause
And not his brother's costly wars;
While Bernadotte would stand as saviour
To his throne in Scandinavia,
Reckoning he'd better lead an
Anti-Bonapartist Sweden.
Britain lived by selling cargo,
So Napoleon sought to block it
By decreeing an embargo
That would hit the British pocket;
Hopeful these 'Berlin Decrees' would now deny all trade
To Britain, so to stop the flow of money that it made –
The money that supported continental coalitions
By paying for the means of war, their armies and munitions.

The Russians [who, until prevented,
Had with Britain traded]
This restriction circumvented –

Or in other words, evaded;
For few were hit so hard by it,
Or chafed as much as they did.

Displeased at this recalcitrance and Russia's non-compliance,
As well to stop the slightest chance of similar defiance,
Napoleon abandoned peaceful courses of persuasion
And launched with half a million men upon a full invasion.
This enterprise, and Russia's size,
Would see NB's undoing:
The summer gone, winter came on,
French casualties accruing.
The Tsar's defeat was not complete, for even Borodino,
Although a blow, was not K O,
As he well knew – and we know.

In Nôtre Dame he'd crowned himself,
A task denied the Pope;
But ten years on, his power gone,
There seemed but little hope.
His enemies thought exile to an island he could run
Would keep him out of mischief, and the way, yet still be fun.
But Bonaparte had known at heart he hadn't had his day,
Though he'd so ignominiously been Elba'd out the way.
Ex-exile, he embarked upon the so-called 'Hundred Days';
His final chance to rally France and General-ly amaze.
His tactical displays, worthy of praise, still weren't enough as,
The day all through at Waterloo, his dreams had hit the buffers.
At journey's end, great hopes a wreck – he'd planned such schemes gigantic…
Years now he'd spend upon a speck of land in mid-Atlantic.

WILLIAM SHAKESPEARE
(1564 – 1616)

'The Swan of Avon', as he's called,
Appears to us as bearded, bald;
No more inclined to show his teeth than
Most who were Elizabethan.
But we cannot say for sure
On evidence of portraiture
That
William Shakespeare appeared thus:
This image that's come down to us
Is based upon one by surmise
Adjudged to be the man we prize,
With subsequently copies done;
But this bloke could be anyone.
Appropriate it is that we
Have such a lack of certainty
About his likeness, since great tracts
Of blanks abound and want of facts
Bestride his life: colossus, yes –
But little's certain; much to guess.

Compared to many of the most important names in History,
The life of William Shakespeare is still something of a mystery.
Already it's been noted that we can't be all that sure
Of what he looked like – as to what he did, and when's, still more
A puzzle to the present, to the future to be passed
As a present passed unopened, as it's been for centuries past –
A little taste of wordplay based
Upon the sort of punny,
Absurd displays that Shakespeare placed
In plays – if not as funny.*

He made his entrance, so they say,
Most aptly, on St. George's Day;
More easily, History accepts it
As that of his final exit.
Born: Stratford, 1564 and died 1616 –
How many writers quite as good as Shakespeare have there been?
Some people might cite Dante, some Cervantes, others Goethe:
Invidious, impossible and unfair to assert a
Supreme linguistic master –
In such matters we are clannish;
'Dante!' cry Italians; 'Cervantes!' shout the Spanish.

* If this stuff irritates and grates,
I'm sorry; I'll endeavour
To keep such whimsy to myself
And not try to be clever.**
** Still worse, this sort of verse,
Which brings complete exasperation
To almost any reader; it's indeed a
Great vexation.

No question, these one rightly sees
As great – they did attain
The highest heights in literature;
One feels, as writers reign,
They all deserve their crown;
But when it's down to finding one
That ranks beside the Bard, it's hard – well, let's be frank, there's none.
For, since he walked the stage, what age
Has not given acclaim
To him most rate the greatest of the greats –
Shakespeare by name?

Anne Hathaway his wife would stay,
He'd go away – she'd cat-sit;
By her his kin's Susanna, twins:
Son, Hamnet, Judith… that's it.

He worked in London in the years from 1592;
Just what he did in the decade before, we've got no clue.
Inevitably, people like to posit their pet notions:
A soldier, some suggest he was, traversing lands and oceans;
He practised Law; he taught; he acted – none at all are verified.
To challenge any/all of the above, do not be terrified.

His writing had engendered envy in a man called Greene
[You'll think the name extremely apt if you've *Othello* seen].
Calling [so it's widely thought] Shakespeare 'an upstart crow',
This ageing thespian, our own age usefully did show –
Although not his intention – in his mention of his writing
That

By 1592, already Shakespeare was exciting
The attention of his fellow dramatists – if some should rate him
'An upstart crow', we know he wrote so well that some could hate him.

The Plague closed all the theatres,
So pragmatically he chose
To concentrate on poetry instead of writing prose.
He scored a hit with *Venus and Adonis*, [which prompts questions
Re. his links with Henry Wriothesley*, and as busily, suggestions].

As actor/ playwright, on the strength of 'The Lord Chamberlain's Men'
['The King's Men', they get called at length, when there's a king again].
The Groundlings found profound things,
And high farce in Theatre's prince:
He had The *Globe* entranced – as he has had it ever since.
Apparently among the rôles he liked to play the most
Was that of Hamlet's father – also known as 'Hamlet's Ghost';
With such a great exponent in a play and rôle self-made,
One might expect a spectre that left others in the shade.

A man of substance presently,
Through writing and investment:
He put his cash in property;
The theatre's where the rest went.
He set up as a Stratford squire,
Acquired a bit of land;
The house he bought was, many thought,
Perhaps the town's most grand.

* Rithszly

104

The name *New Place* it bore –
For sure, a most apt designation;
Still,
As that which it enjoyed, devoid of much imagination.

One story may show something of his humour and his wit:
A theatre-going lady, fancying Burbage quite a bit,
Her feelings had expressed,
Informing him that she preferred
That he come to her made up and dressed
As King Richard the Third.
Will Shakespeare, overhearing,
Then appearing
In his place,
Enjoyed the lady's favours,
Which she gave, as
Shakespeare's face,
Beneath Ricardian paint,
Could only faint-
Ly be discerned;
And not till Burbage turned up
Had the trick he'd pulled been learned.
Will left his calling card –
The lesson: 'William the Conqueror
Did come before King Richard' –
Burbage can't have felt more plonker-er.
It may be quite apocryphal –
The best tales often are –
The truth is still a box chock-full
Of laughs and the bizarre.

To speculate, at any rate,
On many things seems silly;
Likewise to muse upon the views
Of this playgoing filly,
And if she'd pick Burbage's Dick
Sooner than Shakespeare's Willie.

Will's will confounds us still –
Not least in what he left to Anne:
'The second best bed' can be read
As being better than
Nothing at all – but still a small
Bequest for her he'd plighted;
Cut as you may, most scholars say
That Anne was snubbed and slighted.

These days of 'woke', how people spoke
And wrote, for their posterity
Brings tension and dissension –
Both dosed mostly with asperity.
It's nothing new – there's been a few
[Like Pope] who, down the years,
Have felt they must Shakespeare adjust
To better suit their peers.
If some now, vexed by Shakespeare's text,
Should feel on it they must vent
Their criticism in the form of 'sensitive' adjustment,
All well and good – if understood we don't thereby efface
The genius that quite transcends all bounds of time and place.
If all agree, let's wait and see

To tell how far – or whether –
The work we have that's by The Bard
Is not 'Bard' altogether.

MARY SEACOLE
(1805 - 1881)

Mary Seacole was to be a
Force for good in the Crimea;
Though she did a lot before,
It's during the Crimean War
She really made that reputation
Which deserves our salutation.

She herself was not exact
About her date of birth; in fact
Trafalgar had been fought the year
The infant Mary did appear.
Her place of birth: Kingston, Jamaica –
Who'd then guess her life would take her
To such distant points Crimean
So far from the Caribbean?
Mary'd a mulatto mother
And a sister and a brother;
And a Scottish soldier dad,
Who, stationed in Jamaica, had
There come to know her mother well
Through visiting her small hotel.

'Quadroon' in her own day would tend
To be the tag for racial blend
Such as applied in Mary's case –
Her mother being of mixed race.
Mary's Scots blood made her partial,
So she said, to all things martial
[But did not, it seems, impart an
Obvious taste for wearing tartan].

Britain's slave trade ended in her early infancy,
And slavery, officially, in 1833.
'Free-coloureds', though, like Mary, classed themselves with whites; the fact is
Surprisingly, she hardly once passed comment on the practice.
A proudly British subject in the family Imperial,
She'd always seen herself as being of the right material
To make a mark – if not a quid – while nursing others' health;
[Cynics remark that what she did was mainly done for wealth].

From childhood – and her mother – she'd acquired her nursing skill,
Her verve to serve her fellow beings, above all when ill.
And, just like her, entrepreneur and 'doctress'* she would be
[*This 'doctress' word frequently occurred in her biography.]

She got about – for some time out
In Panama, and then,
In London, before heading to Jamaica once again.
She got a bout [you heard it said],
But this time of the cholera;
And though it would leave many dead,
It didn't badly collar 'er.

She had an eight year marriage to an Englishman called Edwin, a
   Union in which she was quite clearly the main breadwinner –
     Nursing him to no avail when he'd succumbed to fever;
As she'd explain, nothing again in life would so much grieve her.

                The powers that be [or were] averse
                   To taking Mary as a nurse
                Had meant her whole Crimean scheme
                Required that under her own steam
                   She get out with least loss or fuss
                   To somewhere near the Bosphorus.

                  Her battle with officialdom
                  Matched soldiers' fighting tales
                  And warrants a comparison
                  With Florence Nightingale's.
                ['The Lady with the lamp' she met,
                   Hoping a nursing post to get;
                   But, for whatever reason, she
                   Could not be used at Scutari].

                 Upon Spring Hill she built and ran
                 From nigh on when the war began
                 A place soon known to many well:
                 The grandly named 'British Hotel'.
This venture needed cash, which Mary's partner did defray,
A man she'd met some years before – a certain Thomas Day.
[Of their precise relationship our knowledge remains slight;
Some more research is needed that on Day may shed more light.
   At present it is fair to say that Day is dark as night].

No pathway evangelical, the one that Mary trod;
Her faith in guava jelly always greater than in God.
When people in despair expected prayer alone to cure them,
She'd wish a greater practical awareness seized a few o' them.

It jars, and mars the record,
But it sadly was the case
That Nightingale saw Seacole as a rival for her place.
She consequently put about some stories to debase her
Within official circles to effectively disgrace her.
'The Lady with the lamp' would stamp
On Mary's share of glory – a
Fact that meant she never went
To tea with Queen Victoria.

Among the tales of Nightingale's:
That an affair had brought her –
That's Mary –
By one Bunbury,
An unacknowledged daughter.
Indeed, a girl named Sally,
Ever pally, called her 'mother';
But that form of address no less
Was used by many another.
So was this Sally Mary's child?
Or might we cite from Oscar Wilde
That Bunbury of Jack's instead
[As useful ill as when he's dead];
The story lacking truthful pith –
The whole thing just an unjust myth?

If Mary had a child, most say
The likely father would be Day.
But if the dad, Day had stayed dumb –
As Mary, so to speak, stayed mum.

In London, growing older she,
Among her 'sons' the soldiery,
Retained respect and great affection
From their earlier connection.
Veterans remembered well
What haven the British Hotel
Had been – none better nor more handy
For a kip, a pie or brandy.

She had shown her patients kindness;
Patience too she's shown
Down all the years in which her contribution's been unknown.
Now, once again respected, not neglected or unseen,
Her bed instead we tend
On History's ward, and Kensal Green.

THEODORE ROOSEVELT
(1858 - 1919)

Forgive me if you know from where
We get the name of 'teddy bear':
Two decades earlier than Pooh –
To be precise, 1902,
The Roosevelt we here present
Under the name of 'Teddy' went,
A nickname-cum-contraction for
His proper name of Theodore.
[For sure, many called Theodore
More than deplore it; by the
Way, they say this 'Teddy' said he
Didn't like it either].

Invited on a bear hunt, he'd not got one,
So to pot one,
His fellow hunters tied one up
So he could say he'd shot one.
All sportsmanship this quite defied,
And Teddy wouldn't do it
[How apt he couldn't *bear* it tried
And that he should *Pooh-Pooh* it!].
All soon aware of 'Teddy's bear',

A firm in celebration
Would launch the toy
That still brings joy
To folk of every nation.
[For safety's sake, though, do not muddle
Real bears with ones you cuddle].

Born to wealth, young Teddy's health
Did not come up to par;
And up to pa it was to see his boy toughened by far
Through a regime of exercise that would comprise a gym;
He had all done to get his son to run and climb and swim.
Weight training and weight gaining,
Teddy set himself a mission,
Transforming his once weak physique
To one in peak condition.

His mother died just hours before the death of his young wife;
His diary records 'the light has gone out of my life.'
Remarried, he'd a brood of five, including his son, Kermit
[No muppet, he – but feel free to check up and confirm it].

Republican, reformist,
The career path he would pave he
Assisted while Assistant
Secretary to the Navy.
Within that post he made the most
Of the tense situation
That did pertain regarding Spain
To bring an altercation.

The fate of the USS *Maine*,
Around which stories grew up,
Brought many theories to explain
Just why the vessel blew up.
As one might guess, the Yellow Press
A war urged undertaking,
With William Randolph Hearst
The worst
For *casus belli*-aching.
Cause of the ship's demise
Defies clear answers; all the same,
In many eyes, the blame
For *Maine*
Falls plainly onto Spain.
Young Teddy saw the coming war,
And keen to see some action,
Swapped office chair for saddle
With a ready satisfaction.
In Cuba he exuberantly rode with the 'Rough Riders' –
Their charge up Kettle Hill rates still among the war's deciders.
The Spanish War brought Theodore a national reputation;
Yet greater fame he soon would claim due to assassination.
McKinley shot, his young Vice got to be the youngest President;
He holds the record still as the White House's youngest resident.
For sure, young Teddy saw
His late chief's killer as a right louse,
Although admitting but for him
He'd not have got the White House.

A man of strong convictions, he was not what you'd call tepid
In anything he undertook – undoubtedly intrepid.
A big game hunter, writer too – indeed, once he'd been keener
To stick to authorship than the political arena.
It's just as well he didn't – that's not meant in a condemning way –
But if he had, we'd simply mix him up with Ernest Hemingway.

He took on Trusts, [though not 'on trust']
The likes of J.P. Morgan;
Big business cried such thrusts
Showed party principles he'd foregone.
'Republican' was no more than,
For Roosevelt, a label:
Enough a man do what he can,
As well as he is able.

To guide his foreign policy,
A hunting tag he'd pick:
i.e. that one speak softly,
But should carry a big stick.
The Panama canal took more than civil engineering –
Of law the scheme fell foul without Colombia first clearing
The project.
As one might expect, young Teddy wasn't ready
To let such technicalities get in the way – instead he
Would back a Panamanian revolt
As a solution –
Then went ahead, result of a successful revolution.

The 1912 election he'd contest without success;
He stood as a Progressive, but had failed to progress.
He'd then gone up the Amazon,
For two years quite a hermit.
He didn't take his wife –
Just a few bearers; also Kermit.

He'd sound credentials green:
He was among the first promoters
Of nature conservation, setting up in the Dakotas
Two of the five great National Parks
That thanks to him exist –
The visionary decision
Of a world philanthropist?
[We may suppose that Kermit, like his father, had been 'green' –
Despite his name, not in the same way some might think he'd been…]

With war once more upon the air,
His nostrils with its scent a-flare,
He thought he ought to be out where
The action was, in France.
Despite the 'bully' use he felt
He might have been, for Roosevelt
Firm backing was quite lacking,
So the scheme did not advance.
A 'bully show', you ought to know, means something 'very good'.
This 'bully pulpit' phrase of his is much misunderstood:
A 'bully pulpit' isn't one of threat, force or invective;
It means you're in a place that helps your case to be effective.
In Teddy's daily speech the 'bully' word was often heard.

[The idea 'bully beef' would beat you up is quite absurd!]
Constraints of time dictate that I'm
Not able here to gush more;
Likewise of space. In any case,
His face is on Mount Rushmore.

CATHERINE THE GREAT
(1729 – 1796)

Who'd have thought that young Sophia
Would in future come to be a
Ruler of a mighty state
And one acclaimed 'Catherine the Great'?
A German princess, not that rich,
She wasn't of a background which
Might prompt a ready expectation
She'd be ruling *any* nation.
So at birth few could have seen her
As a possible Tsarina;
Let alone, once that, one who
Would take the top job in a *coup*.
An empress and an autocrat?
No, no one had expected that.

Her feckless spouse, descended straight
[As grandson] from Peter the Great,
She did her best to interest the immature Karl Peter.
He'd sooner play at soldiers, though, than with his bride
In bed beside.
[His overpowering impotence would finally defeat her].

With conscientious effort, she'd conceived,
But twice miscarried –
The pregnancies of course achieved
Without the man she'd married.
[A courtier, Saltykov, it's thought,
Had done the honours here –
And 'having heirs' one really ought,
As any good courtier].

A daughter died; she then had Paul –
Just one surviving child in all.
[In view of how much grief he caused
Her later on, she might have paused
Before acclaiming his arrival
And the little brat's survival].

Prussian over Russian things
Her husband Peter rated;
Once Tsar, this Peter'd not been great so much as he had grated.
Among his Russian subjects there could not be any doubt
Once Peter's reign came in,
They'd hoped it might soon peter out.

The *coup* caught Catherine on the hop,
No time to stop and worry
About her hair – she was aware
Success meant she must hurry.
Although the explanation she might give would be a fair one –
'Events just moved so fast, I hadn't time to get my hair done' –
While on her way to Petersburg, by luck it did occur

She met coming the other way the coach of her coiffeur.
The *coup* was carried through:
One action taken in a sense key
To its success – she'd dress as guard in the *Preobrazhenski*.
Tsar Peter quit the throne, it's said, 'just like a child led to bed' –
If only he had been instead so biddable when lately wed!

No longer needed any more,
The Tsar, it is inferred had
On Catherine's say so – it's not sure –
Been dealt with – i.e. murdered.
Once on the throne, she made it known
That power would be hers alone.
She'd talk things over, certainly;
But in deciding, only she
Would be the one who gave the nod:
Potemkin? No – Not even God.

Her school reforms defied the norms
When they in ways un-Hunnish went,
They brought surprise to western eyes
By banning corporal punishment.
A child of the Enlightenment,
She always hoped to silence
Those claiming Russia only meant
Barbarity and violence.

She oversaw a lengthy war,
Result of which would be a
Prize that eluded Tsars before:

Control of the Crimea.
She'd clearly here at any rate
Peter the Great
Outclassed;
But conquests of this sort
Now ought
To be things of the past.

The *Hermitage* is by and large the Empress's creation;
Her private art collection would become that of the nation.
Some thought she bought too much,
Fearing her spree would be unending;
Eventually, she would agree, their worries apprehending,
And switched from spending in her reign
To reining in her spending.
Among the plums for generous sums
On which she got her hooks,
Sir Robert Walpole's paintings
And her good friend Voltaire's books.

Progressive and astute,
When smallpox faced her and the nation,
She'd an
Englishman recruit
To oversee inoculation.
Her prompt response in this case wants
For nothing – thus surprising
Her di-la-to-ry mi-li-ta-ry one to an uprising:
The *Pugachev* Rebellion –
Much as Catherine really oughtn't,

She'd failed to see its gravity –
First thought it unimportant.
Like all who'd rule in Russia,
It was vital she should crush a
Challenge of this sort to law and order
On her native turf;
It sounds as if Canute and she
Would very likely disagree
Respecting their capacity
To regulate the serf…

Prodigious Catherine's appetite
For all things intellectual –
While certainly its equal quite,
Those cultural and sexual.
The target of the satirist for her 'unsated lust',
Such barbs at their unflattering-est are very far from just:
Enduring, true affection to her favourites she accorded,
Who for their handsome services were handsomely rewarded.
The palaces apart, the custom grew – as all had been aware –
That when the fling was through, they'd get a set of silver dinnerware.
Count Orlov was among the most important men she'd love
And count a good deal more than some – or 'Orlov' – the above.
Uniquely though, Po*tem*kin
Earned her lasting adoration –
And indeed, some had thought *them* kin
From their close association.

If animal her passions, it at least as much is true
She'd a passion for her animals [let's keep it clean, thank you].

127

Apart from riding horses [in a sense that won't offend],
She doted on her greyhounds – for the breed setting a trend.
Describing herself 'fat and merry' in her later years,
Though sometimes down when old friends died,
She quickly dried her tears.
The paradox presented is indeed one hard to figure:
Although Russia was very big,
Catherine was somehow bigger.

LUDWIG II OF BAVARIA
(1845 - 1886)

Where fairy story castles are concerned, what could be fairy-er
Than Neuschwanstein in its design? It's Disneyland, Bavaria!
The king who thought that just this sort
Of building was a good gig
Was the eccentric monarch
Known to many as 'Mad Ludwig'.

Fantasist, romanticist – a spendthrift some decried,
Of course, his castles now are sources
Of tremendous pride.
Whatever cost and money lost and criticisms made,
These 'follies' now prove quite a wise move re the tourist trade;
And any debt they've long since met and easily repaid.

A Wittelsbach and handsome, Ludwig would be prone to vanity;
But, scion of a family well-known for its insanity,
That madness might afflict him in due course there was a chance –
It certainly was manifest in one of Ludwig's aunts.
Although it is the stuff of farce, this relative attested
A grand piano made of glass she somehow had ingested.
If once unwell, how could one tell who should be summoned sooner –
A doctor, a psychiatrist… or a piano tuner?

Pfistermeister, Pfordten – these
Were Ludwig's minister grandees;
Never to be ones he'd prize as
Very welcome key advisers.
[Private reference saw them go
By the contractions 'Pfi' and 'Pfo',
Such names suggesting they might sing
As extra giants in the *Ring*:
Two of a trio – still to come,
The third, inevitably 'Pfum' …?]

None could contest the claim that
Wagner awed him, and the flame that
Lohengrin would so enkindle
Would endure and never dwindle.
Tristan and Isolde saw
The prince transported even more;
Ludwig very seldom missed an
Opportunity to see
Performances of *Tristan* –
Quite its foremost devotee.

So…
On reading Wagner's pleading
That his music needed backing,
And
Longing for the date on which a patron [so far lacking]
Would show his hand and understand,
In head as well as heart,
The service he might render

As the champion and defender
If he only would extend a
Prop to Holy German Art,
The words at once succeeded –
No more needed
To convince
Young Ludwig
That he could big
Help provide were *he* that prince.
[Had it been written then, well might
Delight make Wagner hum
From gratitude – and from 'Snow White' –
Some Day my Prince will Come].

Was Wagner's gain Bavaria's loss?
In Munich, so they thought;
His rescue by their regal boss
Was far too dearly bought.
The peacocks, silks and velvet suits
That Wagner claimed he needed
All obvious grounds
And reasonable bounds
Had far exceeded.
The Treasury and populace
A common front would show,
And Ludwig had the fact to face
That Wagner had to go.
[He would, of course, be back one day –
And Ludwig missed him while away;
By rights, Bayreuth's a monument

To all that Ludwig's help had meant].

Though tighter fist there might exist
Than that of Pfistermeister,
Still Ludwig wished he would desist
From proffering advice to
Save the kingdom's finances by sprees like these soon ending,
And change such spending in his reign to reining in such
spending.
[Yes, this device has been used twice
Within this same collection;
But as it's apt, and can't be capped,
Indulge, please, its selection].

Though not eschewing wooing,
On his doing so, a hex –
He didn't get that far
With members of the female sex.
Perhaps he wasn't all that keen –
He certainly stayed single;
With likely brides upon the scene
He mostly didn't mingle.
Rooms with women and with him in
Witnessed little action –
To the few of them he knew,
He showed little attraction.
His ministers and people
Hoped their young king would be wed,
If only to see someone that might stand in Wagner's stead.
The Princess Sophie, 17 –

A Wagner fan as well! –
The likely trophy seemed, and queen –
But that scheme didn't gel.
Foredoomed to certain failure,
Ludwig's tale, you're
Going to say?
His subsequent relationships might argue he was gay.
The letters so effusive and indicative of love
He wrote Wagner aren't conclusive, though,
Of that mooted above:
The nature of the friendship that he had with the composer
Was hero-worship – in no guise would otherwise come closer.

Increasingly, Ludwig would be
From state affairs more distant;
To modern life and Munich he
Had always been resistant.
Still more now than before he found a chore
His royal duties,
And obligation to the nation,
Which would never suit his
Romantic temperament –
Which meant him
Solely for Earth's beauties.

Demands of state would soon dictate
His throne should be surrendered;
With him, plea for economy
No bonhomie engendered.
It's clear, for fear tomorrow bring

More borrowing
And debt,
Upon its course of ousting him
The Cabinet had set.

Just how he died we cannot tell –
We're left now to concoct a
Convincing tale of what befell
'Mad' Ludwig and his doctor.
A walk they'd take beside the lake,
The last they'd make – their bodies
Were later found – none else around;
The whole thing very odd is.
Though not aware what happened there
At Starnberg, still depend,
What's true, though out of view,
May well be just around the bend.

ALFRED HITCHCOCK
(1899 - 1980)

Horror's not the *genre* which
His more than fifty films enrich;
But 'gory' is among the words
One *could* use to describe *The Birds*.
Another it might partly fit
Is *Psycho*, although really it
Is – as it ought by name suggest –
Specifically of interest
Through skilfully presenting *traits* a classic psychopath displays.

Distinctive in appearance and in accent as you get,
'Hitch' came to be identified by just his silhouette.
His theme you know – by Gounod:
He would waddle onto set
To a
Tune they call
*The Funeral
March of a Marionette.*

His cameos – most know of those –
Where Hitchcock finds a niche
In every movie,
Go to prove he

More than had an itch
For irony and comedy –
In *Lifeboat* he's an ad.:
The man 'before' [and after?]
Weight loss treatment has been had.
A paradox that while a film might go without a *glitch*,
It never went – and wasn't meant to be – without a Hitch.

The family plot he'd got beyond the studio lot
Had been
Serene – at least compared with what
He dished up on the screen.
[His daughter, Pat, some might know that
In *Psycho* had her hour;
More lucky she than Janet Leigh…?
She doesn't take a shower].

A stocking has a shocking use in *Dial M for Murder* –
Becomes Grace Kelly's would-be noose…She's facing death,
Fighting for breath…Throughout, her husband heard her.
From Madeleine Carroll's shapely leg
A stocking, too, is rolled –
The Thirty-Nine Steps, I'd beg
To say, is cinematic gold;
Upon the screen it's never been
As brilliantly told .*

* [It's all quite clean, this classic scene – no kinkiness be read
Into
Her and Robert Donat's being handcuffed on a bed].

In view of two examples, might his title we amend as
Not 'Master of Suspense' so much as 'Master of Suspenders'?

The 1950s would bring forth
Those films most think his best;
Hitchcock's career was clearly headed North
Rather than West.
The dizzy heights of *Vertigo*
Was cinema sublime;
Some critics further were to go –
'The best film of all time'.
Composer complementary
Hitch had found in Bernard Herrmann –
[New Yorker born, of Russian-Jewish roots – he wasn't German].
His music and the narrative so perfectly do marry;
A Hitch film without Herrmann's like a 'Bond' without John Barry.
With each successive triumph it was harder to be firm on
To whom were due the laurels – which? To Hitch, or more to Herrmann?
Fear, so it's said, that Herrmann's fame
Might less than well impact him,
Detracting from his own great name –
From jealousy, Hitch sacked him.

His directorial *chutzpa*
An acute spur
To a few – though
None more than for French cinema's *New Wave*
And François Truffaut.
A complex man, more complex than
A few he put on screen,

His wide imagination ran
From childlike to obscene.
Possessive and obsessive,
Others' lives in some respect
Were the playthings of his fantasies,
To script and to direct.
Notorious his lechery;
Of tall, cool women blonde,
Without marital treachery,
He could be over-fond.
More fame he brought the famous face
That he might choose to take;
Or, as in Tipi Hedren's case,
One whose career he'd make.
His protégée, she wouldn't play
The part chosen by Hitch –
Which off the screen
Meant she'd have been
No more than Hitch's bitch.

While well aware Bel Air was where
He breathed his last,
At heart,
He'd always be the Londoner
That he'd been at the start.
The London sights of *Frenzy,*
If not all in childhood's guise,
Were nonetheless old friends he
Knew –
With which he had strong **ties**.

His dad had been a grocer,
So it's no surprise that he
Wished Covent Garden put on film
And for posterity.

Among the better-known of his sayings, there's one that'll
A good few thespians annoy: to 'treat actors like cattle'.
With Hitch, though, one must understand
There's always wicked mirth –
He'd have them eating from his hand,
And milked for all their worth.

An Oscar never would be his,
A fact often deplored –
That's show biz!
Genius mayn't win an Academy award.
Besides, they're often given
To the worthy, not the fun;
And though his films could well be both,
You can't please everyone.
With light and dark divided starkly
As two separate schools,
So Hitch's pictures, though they'd sell,
Thus fell between two stools.
If Hitchcock, one's inclined to bet,
Had been a little drearier,
There's every chance he might have met
The judges' strict criteria.
Directors' plaudits still he takes;
And all sincere adherents

Know well the moments when Hitch makes
His cameo appearance. *
The Hitch *aficionado* will
Point to the pioneering skill
Which Hitch so richly had displayed
In the pre-talkies that he made.
So great the later movies, we
May overlook too easily
How much he did to break new ground
Before *Blackmail*, his first with sound.

In turning down a CBE,
Perhaps he gave offence;
For Knighthood consequently
He'd to master his suspense.
Unerringly he'd spot a shot,
In mind's eye, in his gut –
The picture which you're glad you got –
Lights! Camera! Action! …Cut!

* [For those who care to take the time,
'Hitchcock' is hidden in this rhyme;
The letters needed all conform
To a strict pattern – not the norm
Of an acrostic though, it's true;
But here's a helpful final clue:
As in his movies Hitch preferred
Quite early on they slot him,
So likewise here this has occurred –
Now see if you can spot him!]

AUTHOR BIOGRAPHY

The author took a degree in History some time ago but has still not returned it. He lives in Suffolk, where much of his time is spent railing, chafing and sadly shaking his [one] head at most of what he sees and hears.

ILLUSTRATOR BIOGRAPHY

Claire Venables is a designer and illustrator working in the cultural heritage sector. She holds a master's degree from UCL and her work is displayed in museums and heritage sites around the world.